C000182712

GO
CAMPING

GO CAMPING

Text by Katherine Latham, with some text by Phoebe Smith

An Hachette UK Company
www.hachette.co.uk

Summersdale Publishers Ltd
Part of Octopus Publishing Group Limited
Carmelite House
50 Victoria Embankment
LONDON
EC4Y 0DZ
UK

www.summersdale.com

Printed and bound in China

ISBN: 978-1-80007-178-0

Substantial discounts on bulk quantities of Summersdale books are available to corporations, professional associations and other organizations. For details contact general enquiries: telephone: +44 (0) 1243 771107 or email: enquiries@summersdale.com.

GO CAMPING

Discover New Adventures in the Great Outdoors

KATHERINE LATHAM

summersdale

CONTENTS

INTRODUCTION

We live in a time of constant connectivity: always in demand, always available at the click of a button. Why not ditch the strains of modern life and head off camping?

Many of us feel drawn to the wilderness. Camping lets us escape the banality of everyday life and get back to the basics of cooking, exploring, breathing fresh air and just *being*.

Camping is, and always will be, an adventure. There is an element of the unknown that will give you a buzz – including sounds of nature in the depths of the night and pitch darkness outside your little bubble of lamplight. Immersing yourself in the elements in this way can be a truly freeing experience.

Rediscover your spark. Play, laugh, sing. Embrace your inner child and take time to enjoy the little things. Feel the cool air on your face when you unzip your tent first thing in the morning. Run your fingers through the dewy grass. Hear birds chatter as trees sway in the wind. Listen to the crackle of the campfire and watch as the embers dance in the starry night sky. Feel the warmth of your thick socks and woollen blanket, and the heat of the fire on your face as night begins to fall.

Rekindle relationships with the ones you love most. Work together to set up camp, build fires and cook over an open flame. Take your friends, your lover, your children, your dog – or just go alone. Whatever you choose, you'll make memories that will last a lifetime.

Live the life humans are built for. We are wild animals who belong outdoors. This book will help you get back to nature, find the courage to break out of the norm and experience the world as it should be experienced.

Look outside, the wilderness is calling you. What are you waiting for? Pack up and go camping!

THE JOY OF CAMPING

There is so much joy to be found in camping. You can choose your perfect spot, with the perfect view. Set up your tent and roll out your sleeping bag, then kick back and get ready to make lasting, happy memories.

Even just a day or two in the great outdoors is enough to reset. Getting off grid and going with the flow, with none of life's usual ties, frees the mind. Let yourself be governed by daylight, eat good food cooked over an open fire and bathe in the wonders of nature. There really is nothing better for the soul than camping.

TOP TEN REASONS TO GO CAMPING

Camping truly is a life-affirming experience. Here's why...

You get to wake up without an alarm clock. Surrounded by natural light, you rise when the sun does. It's also perfectly acceptable to go to bed when it gets dark, meaning many hours in bed, so you wake up feeling refreshed.

Sleeping bags are so snuggly. There's no scientific reason to explain this, but why is it that settling down inside a sleeping bag is so much cosier than a duvet?

It's a chance to have a campfire! After a day of walking or having outdoor adventures, you can reward yourself with a cosy evening round the fire before curling up inside your sleeping bag (see above).

You'll meet like-minded people. Socializing with fellow campers is what it's all about! From conversations about the latest tent models to simply sharing a mallet to hammer your pegs in, camping will bring you together with some wonderful people.

Visitors of the wild variety may drop by. Sleeping in the outdoors means wildlife will literally be on your doorstep.

From rabbits to foxes, birds to bats, you'll always have guaranteed "wild nights out" when camping.

You have an excuse to leave your phone at home. Embrace the fact that some campsites are off-grid and that camping will give you the chance to reconnect with the natural world. It's time to set your Facebook status to "completely happy" and enjoy!

Stars will always beat any ceiling. It's amazing how a night spent gazing at the blanket of constellations up above can remind us just how big the world is... and how lucky we are to be in it.

It's cheap! Once you've made the initial outlay of buying your kit, you suddenly have the chance to sleep in some of the best places in the world for the smallest of price tags.

It can be as mild or as wild as you'd like. Just because you're outdoors, it doesn't mean you have to be Bear Grylls. If you want to bring everything plus the kitchen sink – do it. Equally, if you want to go super-light and wild-camp in the hills – do it. The choice is always yours.

You start to realize the best things in life aren't "things". When you're watching that sunset or talking to your family and friends, minus the distraction of smartphones, TV or anything else, you'll really begin to appreciate the wonderful world around you.

THE MAGIC OF CAMPING

Camping fact: in 2013, the University of Colorado studied the effects of artificial light on the human body clock. They monitored a group of people who were exposed to a normal (small) dose of outdoor light plus indoor lighting every day for a week, and then got the same group to camp out for a week, with natural light only (no electric lights were allowed). They found that when people's body clocks were synchronized with sunrise and sunset, they experienced better physical and mental health than when they weren't, which explains why camping makes us happy, even when it rains...

For the mind disturbed,
the still beauty of dawn
is nature's finest balm.

EDWIN WAY TEALE

CAMPING AND WELL-BEING

We all know that being outdoors and getting active in the fresh air makes us happy, as well as keeping us fit and healthy. But did you know it can also help you live longer, sleep better, improve your memory and even boost creativity? With camping, you get to heal your soul, move your body and feel truly alive. Here's how...

FRESH AIR

Studies have shown that our bodies benefit from the extra oxygen found in the great outdoors. Not only that, but fresh air is also shown to lower blood pressure, help digestion and boost your immune system.

REDUCED STRESS

As many sites are situated in remote areas, when we pitch camp we often find ourselves cut off, with no phone signal or Wi-Fi. This gives us time to switch off and reconnect with nature. We also have more mental space to think creatively and our stress levels are lowered, which, in the long term, can increase lifespan.

SUNLIGHT

The extra melatonin you get from the huge amounts of natural light you're exposed to as a camper has been shown to improve your mood, with campers consistently reporting feeling happier than non-campers.

ACTIVITY

Even putting up a tent will get you moving! Plus, as there's only so long most of us can sit still inside a tent with the outdoors right on our doorstep, most campers are more physically active. This improves both heart and lung health.

YOSEMITE NATIONAL PARK, CALIFORNIA

The giant rock formations of Half Dome and El Capitan tower over the dense pine forests of Yosemite Valley, deep in the Sierra Nevada mountains of Central California.

There are 13 campgrounds inside the park. Choose from North Pines on the shore of Mirror Lake, or White Wolf, surrounded by towering mountains. For seclusion, opt for Porcupine Flat. This tranquil site is close to Yosemite Falls, one of the tallest in the world, that plunges almost 800 metres (2,625 feet) onto the rocks below.

Feeling really wild? With a permit, head off on an overnight hike and camp deep in the wilderness.

TYROL, AUSTRIA

In the heart of the Austrian Alps, Tyrol is truly wild. With uninhabitable mountainous terrain covering almost 90 per cent of the region, Tyrol is home to more than 500 peaks that tower over 3,000 metres (9,800 feet), as well as spectacular glaciers, lush green meadows and crystalline lakes.

In summer months, hiking and rock climbing are popular, and Tyrol's villages, towns and regions are famous for their traditional customs and celebrations.

In Innsbruck, Tyrol's historical capital city, you can enjoy urban sophistication, while the surrounding Alpine playground boasts around 90 campsites. These range from simple rural sites to luxury camping resorts where you can enjoy an array of spa, sports and recreational facilities.

KNOW
BEFORE
YOU GO

There are a few things you'll need to consider in order to camp like a pro. A bit of preparation before you go will make your camping experience all the more enjoyable when you get there. Think about the gear you'll need, as well as how much you can carry if you're hiking. What facilities are there at your campsite? Is there a shop or café on-site? Plan your meals. Look at the area. Is there a town nearby with a supermarket, pharmacy or hospital? And don't forget to check the weather forecast. You don't want to get caught short without your waterproofs! This chapter details everything you need to know before you go, so you can head off on your camping trip with confidence.

DIFFERENT TYPES OF CAMPING

Camping can be anything you want it to be, from rough, tough and wild to pure luxury. Bivvy up and sleep under the stars, or get cosy in the back garden with your mates in a pop-up tent. Pick a campsite with a bar and live music, or luxuriate in a fully furnished, pre-erected en-suite yurt. The choice is entirely yours.

CAMPSITE CAMPING

Campsites provide an affordable way to holiday. Great for first-timers and families, they range from a handful of tents to sprawling canvas cities. Larger sites often have swimming pools, bars, sports activities and on-site entertainment.

GLAMPING

Popular with couples, glamping (glamorous camping) equals camping in real comfort. Yurts, pods or cabins are furnished with proper beds, fully equipped kitchens and are often en suite. Slow cook on a wood-burning stove and eat at a table with real cutlery.

WILD CAMPING

Do you want to get back to nature with no interruptions? If it's adventure you seek, head into the wilderness with your bedroll on your back.

CARAVANNING

Caravanning has the added bonus of being a home from home. You can make it your own and then take it anywhere. Carry your equipment with ease, not forgetting toys, board games and bikes. Want to bring the kitchen sink? With caravanning, you can.

WHAT YOU WILL NEED

There's nothing worse than setting up camp only to find you've forgotten your sleeping bag! Consider everything you'll need for a successful trip, including bedding, cooking equipment and food, clothes for day and night, protection from the weather, navigation equipment, a torch, spare batteries and washbag essentials. It's a good idea to make a checklist with a section for each category, to ensure no essentials are left behind. The following pages list everything you might need on your adventure.

BASIC ITEMS

- ▲ Tent
- ▲ Spare tent pegs
- ▲ Groundsheet
- ▲ Mallet/hammer (to knock tent pegs into the ground)
- ▲ Swiss army knife
- ▲ Duct tape (useful for almost any emergency)
- ▲ Backpack and daypack
- ▲ Sleeping bag (double up with two sleeping bags if you're going somewhere cold)
- ▲ Pillow (save space by taking a blow-up pillow or simply use a jumper)
- ▲ Warm waterproof jacket
- ▲ Mobile phone and charger
- ▲ Map
- ▲ Guidebook
- ▲ Earplugs (if it's your first time camping, you might find your senses are overactive at night)
- ▲ Torch/head torch (plus spare batteries)

- Bin bags (picking up all your rubbish is the number-one camping rule)
- String/cord (to use as a makeshift washing line)
- Food and drink
- Lightweight stove/barbecue
- Gas/charcoal (remember to take firelighters if using charcoal)
- Matches/lighter
- Saucepan(s)
- Bowl(s)/plate(s)
- Cutlery
- Water bottle
- Water filter or treatment tablets
- Washing-up bowl and washing-up liquid

- Washing-up cloth and tea towel
- First aid kit
- Biodegradable soap
- Antibacterial gel
- Biodegradable wet wipes
- Toilet roll
- Travel towel (these take up less than half the room of a normal towel and dry more quickly, too)
- Toothbrush and toothpaste
- Sun cream

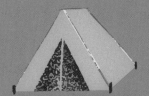

CARS AND CARAVANS

If you're travelling by car or camper van, or taking a caravan, you can afford to pack a few extras that will make your stay all the more comfortable. You might want some binoculars, books or board games. Things that make life easier include comfortable chairs, a fold-up table, a camping stove and a kettle for that cuppa first thing in the morning. You might even want to take a camp bed if that's what makes you happy. Because that's what it's all about – making you happy. If it's comfort you're after, go ahead and pack those luxuries.

EXTRA ITEMS:

- Driver's licence (if you're behind the wheel)
- Sleeping mat/airbed (for a comfier night's sleep. Don't forget the pump if taking an airbed)
- Tarp/sunshade
- Windbreak (for privacy)
- Foldable chairs and table
- Electrical extension cord

- Kettle
- Lantern
- Kitchen utensils
- Cool box/cool bag
- Tin opener
- Hand mirror
- Insect repellent
- Lantern
- Bike(s)

- Bike rack
- Trekking poles
- Umbrella
- Games and books
- Camera
- Binoculars
- Star chart

SOMETIMES ALL YOU NEED
IS TO CLIMB A SIMPLE HILL,
TO SPEND TIME STARING AT
AN EMPTY HORIZON, TO JUMP
INTO A COLD RIVER OR SLEEP
UNDER THE STARS... TO REMIND
YOURSELF WHAT MATTERS MOST
TO YOU IN LIFE.

Alastair Humphreys

CAMPING WARDROBE

The clothes you pack will very much depend on the time of year you're camping, as well as the weather forecast, terrain and part of the world you're heading to.

▲ In warm weather, wear white or pale clothing to reflect the heat and keep you cool.

▲ Take some headgear – a baseball cap, mid-brimmed hat, or even a headscarf or neck warmer can help protect your head from the sun.

▲ Avoid denim – it absorbs heat and takes a long time to dry if it gets wet (really not ideal for camping!).

▲ If the weather will be warm, wear natural or moisture-wicking fabrics (such as cotton, linen, bamboo or polyester), to help increase the airflow to your skin. Loose-fitting outfits will also help your skin stay cooler.

▲ If you're going camping in the winter or somewhere cold, bring double (or even triple) items of clothing. Always take one or two more layers than you think you'll need, to abate any fears of being chilly.

▲ Layer up! For cold-weather camping, your base layer should be tight-fitting to trap heat, as well as moisture-wicking to prevent the absorption and retention of moisture. Your middle layer should be made of either wool or fleece. For your top layer, you'll need a coat or jacket that will provide warmth, as well as acting as a barrier against the rain and wind.

▲ Remember that a lot of heat escapes from the extremities of your body, so don't forget your hat, gloves, scarf (or neck warmer) and thick woolly socks in cold weather!

THE PERFECT SLEEPING BAG

Whether you'll be staying in a sheltered woodland in the balmy summer months or perched on a windswept mountainside, a good night's sleep will get you off to a great start the next day. You'll be able to think more clearly (and will be less likely to suffer injuries if you're off for a day's hiking or other outdoor activity). While it might seem basic, a sleeping bag is actually an important piece of technical gear. There's a lot to consider: the material and filling, the shape and the temperature rating... it's definitely worth doing your research, in order to ensure a restful night. Your choice could make or break your camping trip.

SHAPE: Most sleeping bags will either be rectangular or mummy sleeping bags. While rectangular bags are roomier for your feet – good for those who tend to shuffle around while they sleep – a mummy sleeping bag resembles a cocoon and, as it's more enclosed, it can be warmer.

SEASON RATINGS: All sleeping bags should have a season rating. This tells you what climate the bag is appropriate for. Bags rated "five" are warmer and good for cold conditions, whereas bags rated "one" are better for warm weather.

WEIGHT: Check the weight of a sleeping bag before you make a purchase. If you're going to be doing a lot of hiking and will be carrying it with you, you'll want one that's lightweight.

THE PERFECT BACKPACK

Choosing the right backpack is an important part of planning your trip. Pick a bag that's too big and you'll end up with extra weight to carry. Pick one that's too small and you won't be able to fit everything in. Take your time, try some on and make sure it sits comfortably on your hips, back and shoulders. Choose one made from a hard-wearing weatherproof material, and check for multiple compartments, so you can find the little things with ease. Find your perfect backpack and it will last for years, no matter what you put it through! Here are a few pointers when choosing a backpack...

DON'T IMPULSE BUY: It might be tempting to buy the first backpack you see, or the one that comes up first when you search online, but it's well worth browsing a little longer, so you can be sure you have the right bag for your needs.

QUALITY: A backpack must be comfortable and durable, and it must also fit well. Don't forget, it's going to be carrying your precious belongings and keeping them safe. Generally, you get what you pay for, so if you want something that will fulfil these criteria, it's worth investing in a high-quality bag that you can be confident in. You'll be thankful for it when you're in the great outdoors!

SIZE: While it's important to take note of the size of a bag (which is measured in litres), another good test is to check it's big enough to hold all your kit, while not being too big to carry.

PADDING: You will probably be carrying a lot in your backpack, so make sure it has cushioning on the shoulder straps and hip belt. This helps to reduce the stress that's placed on your body.

WADI RUM, JORDAN

Also known as the Valley of the Moon, the vast desert of Wadi
Rum has a truly other-worldly feel. At dusk, the sun melts over
huge granite rock formations into the rich red sand. Go hiking
or horse riding, watch traditional Bedouin dancing, or simply
be alone with the desert silence. A night at one of the luxury
camps – in a tent fit for Bedouin royalty, or a Martian-style
bubble with a clear view of the star-filled sky – is
truly unforgettable.

RISHIKESH, INDIA

In the foothills of the Himalayas of northern India, Rishikesh sits on the banks of the bright blue Ganges. Near to the source, the river is clear and clean enough to bathe in. Pitch your tent at one of the many riverside campsites, some of which even have a pool or private beach.

The "yoga capital of the world" welcomes visitors from all over the globe who come in search of spirituality. If yoga isn't your thing, there are plenty of high-adrenaline activities on offer, too, including rafting, paragliding and rock climbing.

THE ART OF THE TENT

Ridge, tunnel, dome, geodesic, pop-up, inflatable...
the tent is the star of the show when it comes to
camping – but picking the right one can be a bit of
a minefield. When choosing a tent, you'll want to
consider size, weight and style. If you're off into
the wild, look for a tent that can cope with harsh
conditions. If you're heading to a music festival,
a pop-up is great for a quick-fix pitch. In this
chapter, you'll learn how to pick the perfect tent
that is fit for your adventure.

TENT HUNTING

When you're camping, your tent is your house, so you'll want it to be just right. If you're choosing one for the first time, it can be hard to know where to start. Here are a few tips to help you choose your perfect home away from home... and make it last:

TYPES OF TENT

- ▲ **Pop-up or quick-pitch tents** – these quite literally pop open into a tent-like form. They are convenient, but they're not a good choice for extreme conditions and surroundings.

- ▲ **Inflatable tents** – these have air-filled beams rather than poles, making them quick and easy to pitch. While not recommended for extreme conditions, they're sturdy and reliable campsite accommodation.

- ▲ **Dome tents** – these are easy to erect and a lot taller than traditional ridge tents, but they can be unstable if they don't come with guy lines to tie them down.

- ▲ **Geodesic and semi-geodesic tents** – these are very stable, so it's usually the recommended option for camping trips where you'll be exposed to the elements or sleeping on rough terrain.

HOW MANY BERTHS?

▲ Tents are measured in berths, which refers to the number of people and amount of luggage they can hold. Unless you pack particularly lightly, a good rule of thumb is to factor in two berths per person in the tent – one for the person and one for the luggage!

TENT TOP TIPS

▲ Purchase a groundsheet protector or create a makeshift one with some tarpaulin, pond liner or weed membrane, to protect the bottom of your tent. If you have a tent with a sewn-in groundsheet, pitching will be all the easier.

▲ While your tent is pitched, regularly check that stones or any other sharp objects haven't entered it, as these could rip the groundsheet.

▲ Every time you use your tent, remember to wash the fabric and poles down with soapy water when you're back at home, then let it dry before you pack it away – especially if you've camped near the sea – to prevent corrosion.

TENT HACKS

There are plenty of great tricks that can help you camp like a pro. Here are some top tent hacks that every camper should know for an easy, stress-free trip.

PROBLEM: Hard or saturated ground
SOLVED: Rocks are your friends! If the ground is too tough to drive in a peg, you can either use a rock as a makeshift hammer (be careful) or wrap the guy lines around the rocks and roll them up tight. Then place them on the ground, with two rocks in front of them to anchor them. On very wet ground, a similar technique will work, as long as you have enough rocks to hold the cord in place.

PROBLEM: You've lost your tent pegs
SOLVED: Look for branches with protruding sticks, as these will be easy to use as makeshift pegs (use strong wood, as it will hold things more securely).

PROBLEM: High winds
SOLVED: Use your kit (and yourself)! As soon as you've pitched, put your rucksack inside to act as a weight. Distribute your heaviest kit to each of the corners, to act as extra ballast. If you don't have enough kit for this, use stones. Do remember that once you are safely inside, you yourself will be the best weight to keep your tent in place.

PROBLEM: Guy lines are too short
SOLVED: See what you have to hand and improvise. Your rucksack will have a cord, as will your sleeping-bag "stuff sack".

PROBLEM: Cold weather
SOLVED: Place next day's clothes inside your sleeping bag with you while you sleep, then wake up to toasty warm togs to put on in the morning.

PUTTING UP YOUR TENT

Remember, putting up a tent can be tricky, especially if the wind is blowing, the rain is lashing down and the kids are screaming. So, before you go on your camping trip, try putting up your tent at least once in your garden, so that it's more familiar (and also to check you have all the bits you need). It's much better to struggle with something when there's no audience or pressure!

TENT SWEET TENT...

Taking the basics with you will ensure your tent is comfortable enough, but how do you make it feel like a home from home? Here are a few tips you can try, to make your tent feel extra cosy.

▲ Put up a flag or some bunting – a great way to personalize your space and bring a burst of colour to your trip. It will help you easily spot your tent in a crowded campsite, too.

▲ Consider a "carpet" – whether you take a tent "footprint" (a piece of groundsheet-like material that sits between your tent and the ground, protecting the underside of your tent from wear and tear), a rug or a blanket for the porch, having something warm underfoot will make any tent feel instantly cosy.

▲ Take a pillow – camping shouldn't have to be uncomfortable. Bring an actual pillow and you'll be as comfy as if you were in your own bed.

▲ Light a lantern – head torches are functional, but a lantern is far more cosy! Hang a lantern from your tent to make the space feel like a proper room or, even better, if you have a camper van or caravan, you could string up some fairy lights.

▲ Take a seat – sitting cross-legged on the floor is all well and good, but bringing a camping chair will be much better for your back long term and will get you off the cold floor when the sun sets.

▲ Stay toasty – consider taking a hot-water bottle. Getting into a pre-warmed sleeping bag is an experience that everyone should have. Sleep tight!

MIYAJIMA, JAPAN

Officially named Itsukushima, this mountainous island in Hiroshima Bay is a UNESCO World Heritage Site and one of the best places to camp in Japan.

More commonly referred to as Miyajima, or "Shrine Island", it's home to one of Japan's most famous sights. At high tide, the great "floating" Torii gate of Itsukushima Shrine rises from the sea – a vision not to be missed.

Towering over the bay, Mount Misen is the island's highest peak. Various hiking trails will lead you to the summit, or take the gondola for breathtaking views of the 3,000 islands that dot the Seto Inland Sea.

SARDINIA, ITALY

Sardinia is the second-largest island in the Mediterranean Sea. It has around 2,000 kilometres (1,243 miles) of coastline, with sandy beaches and sparkling blue waters, and the rugged interior is criss-crossed with hiking trails.

The best time to visit the island is between April and June, when the sea is warm, the flowers are in bloom and the cool air of spring still lingers. Many of Sardinia's campsites are located near the coast, so you can enjoy sea views from the eucalyptus grove that shades your pitch.

Be aware, though, that wild camping is strictly forbidden in Sardinia and those who break the rules risk high penalties.

BUSHCRAFT 101

"Bushcraft" refers to the skills and knowledge needed to survive in the great outdoors, with only nature at your disposal. It's about living off the land, using natural resources in a responsible and sustainable manner.

Bushcraft can help us reconnect with our ancestral roots, using ancient techniques and knowledge passed down from generation to generation.

If you've ever picked blackberries to make a crumble, then you've already started your bushcraft journey! Bushcraft skills can include foraging, firecraft, tracking, shelter-building and twine-making. Knowledge of bushcraft can be empowering, giving you confidence when you're out in the wild. This chapter will introduce you to the basics.

HOW TO LIGHT A FIRE

Our ancient ancestors used fire for warmth, protection and cooking and, even in this age of central heating, we are still drawn to those dancing flames. Experts think our fascination with fire is ingrained in us all and contributed to our evolution as a species. While our ape cousins went to sleep with the setting sun, our ancestors would sit around a fire, to contemplate and socialize. Building a fire is an integral part of any camping trip. Here's how to make the perfect campfire.

1. Look for a flat area a few metres from anything flammable, including overhanging trees and your tent!

2. Make your fire bed on exposed earth. If necessary, dig up a patch of grass (when you're done, pop the patch back in, leaving no trace). Place a ring of rocks around the edge to contain the fire.

3. You'll need tinder, kindling and fuel. Tinder is fast-burning – small twigs, dry leaves or needles work well. For kindling, look for sticks about an inch thick. Your fuel will be logs.

4. Keep a bucket of water nearby. Lay out your tinder. If you've brought firelighters (there are plenty of eco-friendly options), pop one in now. Arrange your kindling, criss-crossed over the top. Light your fire! Give it a gentle blow if it's having trouble. Next, add your fuel (being careful not to crush your kindling structure). Keep adding logs as needed, to keep your fire alight.

5. Give yourself plenty of time to extinguish your fire before you turn in for the night. Sprinkle water over the fire and stir the embers with a stick, to make sure it's good and wet.

MAKING FIRE
WITHOUT A MATCH

Starting a fire without a match is a vital skill for any true adventurer. Once you have your tinder – bark, dried grass, fir cones, pine needles, wood shavings or a feather stick (see page 61) – you have a few choices as to how to bring your campfire to life. Try making a few flames with any of the following methods.

SUNLIGHT

WHAT DO I NEED? Any kind of lens – a magnifying glass, eyeglasses or binoculars.

WHAT DO I DO? Angle the lens toward the sun to focus the beam on your tinder, be patient and soon you'll have your fire.

DRAWBACKS: Needs good sunlight. Overcast conditions won't work.

FRICTION

WHAT DO I NEED? A piece of cord, a bendable branch, a soft wooden plank of dead, dry wood (e.g. sycamore, willow or birch), a knife, a hard wooden branch and a rock.

WHAT DO I DO? Make a bow by tying the cord to each end of the bendable wooden branch. In the soft plank – "the fireboard" – use the hard wooden branch to drill a small depression about 2 centimetres (0.8 inches) from the edge. Then, using your knife, cut a V-shaped notch in the centre of the depression. Place your tinder on a leaf or similar (to keep it together), then place this underneath the notch. Grab the hard wooden branch – your drill – and twist it into the cord of the bow, securing one end in the notch in the fireboard so it stands upright. Then start sawing to create friction. In doing so, after much perseverance, you will create embers that will fall down through the notch on to your kindling. Pick them up and blow on them to add oxygen, and you'll get your flame.

DRAWBACKS: It can take time to find the pieces required to build this apparatus – and it takes a fair amount of patience and practice to get this device to work. To be on the safe side, consider carrying a fire steel with you, as this will work to create sparks, no matter what. Even if you find yourself in damp conditions, you should be able to start a fire. They are available from all good camping stores.

HOW TO COOK OVER A CAMPFIRE

Everything tastes better when it's cooked outdoors. You can cook some surprisingly complex dishes over an open fire and there are a few ways to do it. You could place a cast-iron skillet straight onto the fire, or make a skewer from a green (living), non-toxic twig, such as hazel or ash. For a stew, soup or to boil water, you'll need a saw and a cooking pot with a bucket handle.

The echoes of beauty you've seen transpire, resound through dying coals of a campfire.

ERNEST HEMINGWAY

HOW TO MAKE A COOKING STAND

1. Use your saw to cut two Y-shaped branches from a tree, about centimetres thick and a metre long, plus another straight branch, also about a metre long. Make sure the straight branch is green, so it won't burn. This is the one that will hang above the fire.

2. Before you light your fire, drive the two Y-shaped branches into the ground on either side of your firebed, making sure they're firmly stuck in. If you have a mallet or a rock to hand, use it to ram them into the earth until they're stable.

3. Thread the straight branch through the handle of your cooking pot and hang it in the crooks of the Ys. Light your fire and you're cooking!

MAKE YOUR OWN CAMPING STOVE

While cooking on an open fire can feel exhilarating, it also requires frequent maintenance – you need a lot of wood and have to refuel your fire often. If you want an easier option, while still using some of the natural resources around you, why not make your own tin-can camping stove? That way, you don't have to worry about lugging gas canisters around – and you still get to make a fire! With just three handfuls of twigs, you'll have enough fuel to create an efficient wood fire that will boil water in about 8 minutes. Here's how to do it.

1. Take two empty tin cans (lid removed on one end), one small enough to fit inside the other. Make sure they're clean. Remove the labels. Place the smaller can on top of the larger one and trace a circle around it. Cut out the drawn section using sheet-metal shears and file the edge to make it smooth.

2. Turn the large can over and drill two rows of holes around the base. Use a drill bit to enlarge the holes.

3. Take the smaller can and drill holes in the lid, evenly spaced.

4. Drill two rows of holes around the bottom of the small can and a row of holes around the top end, too.

5. Fill your small can with twigs, pine cones or bits of torn-up cardboard. Put the little can inside the big can and light her up! Now, you're ready to cook up a feast.

HOME IS WHERE
MY TENT IS

FINDING WATER

Go without water for a day and your physical and mental strength will be depleted. It becomes difficult to perform essential tasks and the risk of injury increases. You need about 2 litres (3.5 pints) of water per day – and with a bit of know-how, water can be found pretty much anywhere.

HOW TO FIND WATER

Water runs downhill, so follow valleys or ditches downward. Follow animal tracks or birds as they flock toward water in dry areas.

HOW TO COLLECT WATER

Clear, flowing water is the safest option, but if you can't find a stream, there are other ways to collect water. If it's raining, tie the corners of a tarpaulin around trees a metre or two apart, place a small rock in the centre to create a dip and let the water gather. Tie absorbent clothes around your legs and run through long grass to collect dew. Or place a plastic bag over a leafy, non-toxic branch, such as any fruit tree, ash or hazel. Moisture is carried from a plant's roots to its leaves. From there, it usually evaporates... but not if you catch it first.

HOW TO PURIFY WATER

Water can be contaminated with mud, bacteria or pollution. It's a good idea to carry a shop-bought water filter or purification tablets. If you don't have those, fill a clean sock with layers of sand, pebbles, then straw. Filtering your water through this will remove any dirt. Now boil the water for 4 minutes, to kill any bacteria.

WHITTLING AND CARVING

Meditative and repetitive, whittling or carving is perfect for whiling away the hours. Whittling is the art of carving wood using a knife. Carving employs the use of chisels, gouges and other tools. Whittling and carving are not only relaxing, they are useful skills to have when out in the wild. You can make all sorts of things – skewers to cook with, tinder to light your fire, or even tent pegs.

MARSHMALLOW STICK

Cut a green (living) branch from a tree, about 1 centimetre (0.4 inches) round and 50 centimetres (20 inches) long. With your knife, strip shavings off one end. Work your way all the way around, until you have a pointed tip. Pop your marshmallow on the spike and you're ready to roast.

FEATHER STICK

Feather sticks make great tinder. Take a small branch and shave layers away (as with the marshmallow stick), but this time leave the shavings attached at one end. The resulting curls (or feathers) are perfect for burning.

TENT PEG

For a tent peg, you'll need your knife and a camping or folding saw. Find some branches approximately 20 centimetres (8 inches) long and 3 centimetres (1.2 inches) thick. With your knife, sharpen one end of the branch into a point. About 5 centimetres (2 inches) from the unsharpened end, saw about a quarter of the way through the branch. Cut a V shape with your knife, at 45 degrees to the saw cut. This is the notch that will hold your guy line. Round the top of the peg with your knife to stop it splitting when you hammer it into the ground.

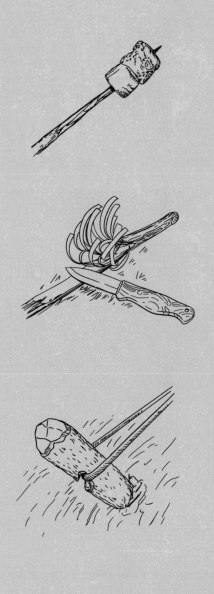

NATURAL NAVIGATION

Natural navigation is the skill of being able to find your way using nature alone as your guide. Navigate by the sun, moon, stars, land, sea, weather, plants or animals – nature will always show you the way. Below are just some of the techniques you can use.

THE SUN

Once you understand the sun's arc, it's possible to use it to determine your direction of travel. In the UK, the sun rises in the north-east in midsummer, the east in spring and autumn, and the south-east in midwinter. North of the Tropic of Cancer, the sun is always due south when highest in the sky.

THE MOON

If there is a crescent moon in the sky, you can pinpoint south. Draw a line from the top tip to the bottom tip, and then all the way to the ground.

POLARIS, THE NORTH STAR

The northern sky can be read like a clock, with Polaris at its centre. The North Star always sits over the North Pole, so will always point you in the direction of north. To find Polaris, draw a line from the two outermost stars of the bucket of the Big Dipper. It will lead straight to Polaris. (See yellow star on diagram.)

MOSS

Moss is quite fussy: it prefers cool, shady conditions, and as such it grows unevenly on the sides of trees. The south side of a tree trunk will naturally receive more sunlight. This means the mossy side of a tree indicates north, while the side free from moss indicates south.

NATURAL FIRST AID

The world is full of natural resources that have the power to heal various ills. Archaeological excavations from 60,000 years ago have found remains of medicinal plants, and it's thought that humans have used plants as medicine for as long as we have existed. Here are a few you might find, and how to use them.

SPHAGNUM MOSS: A favourite of bushcrafters, this green peaty moss has antiseptic properties. If you scratch yourself or get a small cut while camping, this is perfect to clean the wound – simply rub the leaves (which will be watery) over the affected area. It's also great for cleaning out your bowls and cups. Found on boggy ground, it's soft to the touch and can be recognized by its tiny leaves, which can be toothed, grow in tufts close to the stem and are usually light green.

BIRCH POLYPORE FUNGUS: Forgotten the blister plasters? Not to worry. These large white fungus slabs can be found in the woods, growing on rotting trees. They are shaped like shelves and always grow horizontally. Spongy, non-toxic and highly absorbent, birch polypore fungus is naturally cooling, anti-inflammatory and antibacterial, and is also easy to cut into any shape to place directly onto the affected skin.

DOCK LEAVES: Most of us probably used these in childhood – and they're worth remembering. If you get stung by nettles, look out for one of these perennial weeds (always found nearby). The leaves contain a natural astringent, which soothes, and they can also be used on burns and blisters.

LIFE IS GOOD WHEN
YOU'RE CAMPING

AORAKI/MOUNT COOK NATIONAL PARK, NEW ZEALAND

Far from the city lights, stars dust the night sky above Aoraki/Mount Cook National Park in the Mackenzie region of New Zealand's South Island. The National Park is a vast expanse of untouched alpine landscape that boasts dazzling blue lakes, permanent snowfields and 23 peaks over 3,500 metres high (approx. 11,400 feet), including New Zealand's highest mountain, Aoraki/Mount Cook.

Mountaineers say the area has the best climbing in Australasia, while hikers can follow the many mountain paths to alpine tarns, herb fields and stunning glaciers.

There are 17 huts within the park, most for mountaineers with climbing skills. In Mount Cook Village, you can find well-equipped campsites with spectacular views.

CORCOVADO NATIONAL PARK, COSTA RICA

Corcovado National Park is one of the largest tropical rainforests in Central America. The park sits on the Osa Peninsula on the southern tip of Costa Rica's Pacific coast. It is one of the world's most biodiverse regions, home to scarlet macaws, tapirs, jaguars, ocelots and squirrel monkeys.

Here, you can hike across pristine beaches, or head inland through mangrove swamps to lowland and mountainous rainforests.

To get to Corcovado National Park, either take a challenging hike along either one of the jungle or coast-hugging tracks, or catch a boat to the easier tracks around the Sirena and San Pedrillo ranger stations.

THE CAMPING KITCHEN

One of the great joys of camping comes from cooking and sharing food under the stars while your fire crackles away. When you've had a long day outdoors, you'll want a hearty dinner that can be cooked quickly. Why not pre-prepare your first meal, so that after you've found your bearings and pitched your tent you'll be ready to cook with very little effort? Ready-made foil pack recipes are perfect for this. And don't forget to pack some treats! Need a little inspiration? The following pages will help you decide what to bring, as well as detailing some delicious campfire recipes.

THE CAMPSITE KITCHEN

Camping meals have a bad reputation: flavourless, oversalted and watery – the list of faults can be endless. But it doesn't have to be this way. Get some basics packed in your rucksack and you can add a definite *zap* to a meal. From extras, such as olives and sultanas, to herbs, including coriander and oregano, and even baked beans and vegetable/meat stock, there's always a way to make your mealtimes more appealing.

FOR COOKING EASE, REMEMBER TO BRING:

- ▲ Frying pan
- ▲ Saucepan
- ▲ Wooden spoon
- ▲ Tongs
- ▲ Sharp knife
- ▲ Chopping board
- ▲ Scissors

- ▲ Bottle/can opener
- ▲ Water container (you don't want to keep going back and forth to the tap every time you need water so take a large container with you)

If you're travelling with limited supplies and you're refrigerator-free, here's a list of handy key ingredients:

▲ Fruit and vegtables (such as corn on the cob, butternut squash, mushrooms, onions, apples and oranges)

▲ Oats

▲ Pasta, rice, lentils and beans

▲ Canned tuna

▲ Canned tomatoes

▲ Cooking oil

▲ Teabags, instant coffee and hot chocolate (if you have access to a kettle or campfire)

▲ Long-life milk

▲ Water, squash or fruit juice

Heading out to camp in the wild? No room for a full-on campsite kitchen? Not to worry – food is in the bag…

DEHYDRATED: Packaged in a lightweight pouch, this is dried food that you simply add boiling water to and leave for several minutes before digging in (don't forget to remove the freshness crystal sachet before adding the water!). It's definitely the lightest option, but a word of warning: if your stove doesn't work, or you can't source water, you will go hungry.

PRE-COOKED: A heavier option, but the food in these packets is already cooked, so it simply needs heating up, boil-in-the-bag style. The advantage is that, in an emergency, you can resort to eating the contents cold. Yum!

GARLIC HASSELBACK POTATOES

These parcels of delicious, garlicky goodness are the perfect way to refuel and relax after a day in the great outdoors.

INGREDIENTS

4 medium-sized jacket potatoes

Butter or olive oil

Salt and pepper, to taste

8 garlic cloves

1 onion, thinly sliced

Optional: cheese; herbs, such as thyme or rosemary

METHOD

1. First, prick holes in the skins of each of your potatoes using a fork. Then cut slits in the top of each one about halfway down into the potato.

2. Rub olive oil, salt and pepper over the outsides of each potato and place on a piece of foil. Place a whole garlic clove in the slit closest to the centre of the potato, and use an extra garlic clove per potato, thinly sliced, to fill the other slits.

3. Add a thin slice of onion to each slit, then add a drizzle of olive oil or a dab of butter to each.

4. Wrap the foil tightly around each potato and place directly onto the fire for 1 hour, or until soft. Serve with your favourite toppings.

Cooking and eating food outdoors makes it taste infinitely better than the same meal prepared and consumed indoors.

FENNEL HUDSON

ONE-PAN FULL ENGLISH

Making a complete breakfast in a single pan means less washing-up at the campsite sink!

INGREDIENTS (adjust to size of pan/party)

1 tbsp olive oil / knob of butter

2 sausages (or vegetarian equivalent)

2 rashers of bacon
(or vegetarian equivalent)

100 g (3.5 oz) mushrooms

4 eggs

Pepper

6 tomatoes

Handful of grated cheese

METHOD

1. Heat the pan. Add the butter or olive oil until it bubbles, then add the sausages. Leave for about 3–4 minutes, turning frequently.

2. Add the bacon, turning occasionally. Once it's crisping up, throw in the mushrooms, too. Cook until they are almost ready (a further 5–6 minutes).

3. Beat the eggs and stir in a pinch of pepper, then add to the pan, making sure you cover everything, omelette style. Add the tomatoes to the pan, then turn the heat down.

4. Leave for another couple of minutes, then add the cheese on top. After about a minute, the cheese will start to melt. Remove the breakfast from the pan and enjoy!

CHILLI-BEAN NACHOS

You won't even need plates for this moreish dish – simply serve in one sharing bowl.
But be warned – you might end up fighting over the final few chips!

INGREDIENTS

1 tbsp olive oil

1 onion, pre-chopped

1 tin kidney beans, drained

1 red pepper

1 tin chopped tomatoes

1 tsp paprika

1 tsp cocoa powder

Pinch of salt

1 big bag of lightly salted nacho chips

Small jar of jalapeños (optional)

1 pack of grated cheese (Monterey Jack or Cheddar work well – optional)

Fresh coriander plus lime wedges, for serving (optional)

METHOD

1. To make the sauce, heat the olive oil in your pan and sweat the onion until it's translucent.

2. Add the beans, pepper and tinned tomatoes. Stir in the paprika and cocoa powder. Add salt to taste. Simmer until piping hot.

3. Lay the nacho chips out in a wide bowl and pour over the sauce. Top with jalapeños and sprinkle with grated cheese.

4. Serve with a spattering of fresh coriander and lime wedges.

SAUSAGE AND APPLE ONE-POT

This hearty meal is sure to be popular among your famished campsite crew – a one-pot stew that promises to warm your heart, whatever the weather.

INGREDIENTS

1 tbsp olive oil

6 pork and apple sausages (or substitute for vegetarian sausages, if you prefer)

2 apples, halved

1/2 red onion, sliced

1/2 red cabbage, chopped

Salt and pepper, to taste

300 ml (1/2 pint) apple cider

2 tbsp cider vinegar

METHOD

1. Heat the oil in a large skillet. Add the sausages, turning occasionally until golden. Remove the sausages from the pan and put to one side.

2. Put the apples into the skillet, cut side down. Add the onion and cabbage. Stir for 3–4 minutes, until the apples are browned. Season with salt and pepper.

3. Put the sausages back in the skillet, and add the cider and vinegar. Simmer for about 20 minutes, until the sausages are cooked through and the apples are tender.

COLD AIR, DARK NIGHT,
WARM FIRE, BRIGHT STARS

CAMPFIRE-BAKED BANANAS

Baking bananas is so easy that, when you've done it once, you won't look back! Simply add a delicious filling of your choice to make an irresistibly sweet treat. Here are just two topping ideas.

INGREDIENTS

6 ripe bananas

FOR THE FILLING:

6 tbsp honey

6 tsp cinnamon

OR

2 packs chocolate chips
(approx. 30 g or 1.5 oz)

2 handfuls small marshmallows
(approx. 50 g or 1.8 oz)

METHOD

1. Keeping your bananas in their skins, make a slit down one side. With a fork, mash the banana flesh inside the skin. Add a sprinkling of your chosen filling.

2. Wrap each banana in foil and, using tongs, place directly onto the fire.

3. Leave to cook for about 15 minutes, then remove from the fire and leave to cool.

4. Unwrap and spoon your gooey banana delight straight from the foil.

CAMPING SNACKS

Unless you're glamping or caravanning, it's unlikely you'll have a fridge. And even if you're sharing a campsite fridge with other campers on the site, you probably won't have much room. So, it's a good idea to bring plenty of snacks that don't need to be kept cool. Dried, tinned and plastic-wrapped foods are best. Some things can be pre-cooked and will keep for a day. Here are some ideas to keep you well fuelled.

- Bread, rolls or bagels
- Granola bars or energy balls
- Dried fruit
- Fresh fruit (sturdy items, such as apples, pears and oranges)
- Peanut butter and/or jam
- Cold pizza (cooked the day before)
- Crackers
- Dry cereal
- Nuts
- Carrots
- Flapjacks
- Crisps
- Sausage rolls, pies and pasties
- Sugary sweets
- Instant noodles

To me, food is as much about the moment, the occasion, the location and the company as it is about the taste.

HESTON BLUMENTHAL

CAMPFIRE COOKING

If an open flame or burning charcoals are on offer, seize the chance to make your camping cooking more exciting (and your desserts more fun!). Some fireside camping staples include:

BAKED POTATO: You can't go wrong with one of these. Simply wash, pierce with a fork several times, wrap in foil and then throw onto the coals or into the fire. An hour later, you'll have a tasty spud to replace lost carbs.

CORN ON THE COB: Another quick and easy snack. Simply wash, wrap in foil, place on the coals or into the fire and let the flames do the rest. It should take around 10 to 15 minutes to cook. Just don't forget the skewers, or prepare for burned fingers...

MARSHMALLOWS: Simply find a stick (choose an edible tree like pine or apple to make sure it's non-toxic), place a marshmallow on the end and hold over the heat – soon, a gooey treat will await. Best served with a good ghost story or a cheesy guitar rendition of "Kumbaya".

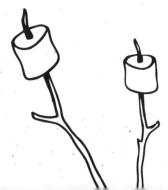

The comforts of life's
essentials — food, fire
and friendships.

JULIA CHILD

FORAGING

For our hunter-gatherer ancestors, foraging was a necessity. For us, it is often done purely for enjoyment. Discovering a hidden world of wild food is one of the simplest and most satisfying ways to immerse yourself in nature.

Eating with the seasons and sourcing food from nature has long been advocated by distinguished chefs and restaurateurs. Food is at its most delicious when it's fresh from the bush, tree or rock pool. And that anticipation of blackberry or wild garlic season – or any other foodie season – makes the dishes that you conjure up all the more memorable. This chapter will introduce you to the basics of foraging, so you can learn what to search for... and when.

HOW TO FORAGE

There are a few things to bear in mind while foraging. It's important to know exactly what you're looking for, as well as where and when things grow. Here are some pointers:

▲ If you're not 100 per cent sure, don't pick it! Some edible plants are almost identical to deadly poisonous ones. For example, wild chervil is delicious, but it looks just like hemlock, a plant that could kill you within hours. Always try a small amount first, even if you're sure you've picked the right thing, just to make sure.

▲ Woodland and hedgerows are great places to start. You'll find hawthorn leaves, nettles, garlic mustard, wild garlic, elder, sloe and blackberries.

▲ Foraging in public spaces and footpaths is allowed. On private land, make sure you get permission from the owner.

▲ Be careful where you forage. Stay away from busy roads, where the leaves might be covered in fumes, and always pick from above hip height if you prefer to avoid dog urine as an added ingredient!

▲ If you find an amazing patch of wild food, be considerate with your picking. Leave some for pollination and for others to forage, and also for insects and animals – don't forget, this may be an important food source for wildlife.

LET NATURE INTO
YOUR HEART, SOUL
AND STOMACH

Wild garlic

Wild garlic – also known as bear leek, bear's garlic, broad-leaved garlic, buckram, ramson or wood garlic – is quintessentially British, a springtime woodland plant. If you ever crunched the leaves underfoot as a child, the scent will likely have stayed with you forever!

If you're new to foraging, searching for wild garlic is the perfect way to start. It's easy to identify, prolific and tasty! Wild garlic loves damp, shady conditions. You can often find it in abundance carpeting the banks of streams and rivers from late winter until the end of spring.

Wild garlic has a more delicate flavour than the bulb garlic you would usually use in cooking. Both the leaves and flowers are edible. Pick the young leaves in March – delicious when added to soups and pasta. And the little white flowers, which bloom from April to June, give a garlic hit to sandwiches and salads.

Or why not whizz up a wild-garlic pesto? Grind together with walnuts, olive oil and grated Parmesan, then toss with cooked pasta. Foraged wild garlic will last a day or two after collecting, so plan ahead for a yummy meal!

Conifer needles

Conifer needles are rich in vitamins A and C. They are fantastic for your immune system and can help to lower blood pressure. Conifers truly are a superfood of the wild – and one that can be foraged any time of year.

Conifers can be found across northern Asia, Europe and North America. In fact, coniferous forests make up one third of the world's forests, so you'll never be far from a conifer tree.

Pine, spruce and fir are all types of conifers – and they are all edible. Pine trees have long needles that grow in clusters of two, three or five. Fir trees have flatter, softer needles. On a fir branch, the needles grow on opposite sides, so the branch appears to be flat. Spruce trees have round, spiky needles that grow from the branch in all directions. With the exception of the yew, all needled conifers are safe to eat. You can recognize a yew by its distinctive red berries and scaly bark.

When foraging, opt for the lighter-coloured needles at the tips of each branch. Younger conifer needles have a more delicate flavour, whereas needles from a mature branch have a strong, bitter taste.

The earthy, herbal flavour pairs well with fish or chicken: simply sprinkle the needles on top and cook in a foil parcel. Alternatively, enjoy as a tea: boil 2 or 3 cups of water and add 4–6 tablespoons of pine needles. Let the needles steep for 10 to 15 minutes. Strain and sweeten with honey to taste.

Blackberries

For many, blackberry picking is a treasured childhood memory. In late summer, when the sun hangs hot and heavy in the sky, there is nothing better than a scramble through a blackberry bush, collecting juicy berries for a crumble or pie, coming home tired and scratched, with purple-stained lips and a tub filled to the brim.

Blackberries are easy to identify and are abundant in late summer and early autumn. By October, damp weather will probably have soiled the crop. Find them in hedgerows, woodlands, along canal paths and across scrubland in the countryside or town.

If you keep your blackberries dry when storing them, they should last for two to three days. The berries freeze well, too, so be sure to collect enough to see you through winter.

Choose carefully. Pick the best-looking berries that are shiny and firm. Use your harvest in pies and crumbles with apples or raspberries. Blackberries are delicious on top of a cheesecake, rolled in a crêpe, or heated with a little sugar or honey and poured over ice cream. These woodland gems also make a great accompaniment for meats, such as venison or pigeon.

BLACKBERRIES CLUSTERED
AGAINST THE SKY, HEAVY AND
DARK AS THUNDER, WHICH WE
PLUCKED AND GOBBLED, HOUR
AFTER HOUR, LIPS PURPLE,
HANDS STAINED TO THE WRISTS.

Laurie Lee

Dandelion

From May to October, the familiar sunshine faces of dandelions spring up everywhere – in meadows, fields, parks, gardens and even gutters. These plentiful little treasures are so incredibly versatile, it's hard to believe we usually view them as weeds.

The dandelion is a perennial herb, with a long list of culinary and medicinal uses. All parts of the dandelion are edible, from the flower to the leaves to the root – although the fluffy seeds would be less than pleasurable to consume!

It's easy to find dandelions. They grow in all seven continents of the world and thrive in many different climates. Pick dandelion flowers late in the morning or in the afternoon, when the blooms are completely open and dry. The leaves are best harvested in early spring. When picking, opt for the biggest leaves with the fewest lobes, as they're the tastiest.

Dandelion greens are highly nutritious, brimming with vitamins, folate, iron and calcium. The leaves are a great peppery addition to any salad, or team with lemon to whip up a zingy pesto. The leaves can be cooked in the same way as spinach or spring greens. Sauté in olive oil, season with salt and pepper, and add a squeeze of lemon. The flowers are sweet and great for making jelly, mead and tea.

Fennel

For a quick burst of flavour, search for fennel. It can be identified by its fleshy stems and a spray of lace-like yellow flowers – if you squash the stem and smell liquorice, you've found it.

Wild fennel is prolific in the UK and is often considered a pest. It is usually found near the coast, in fields and on roadsides. Throughout the summer months, once you know what you're looking for, you'll start seeing it everywhere.

Wild fennel has many medicinal properties and is a great digestive. It has a strong smell and tastes of anise or liquorice. When foraging, you want the fronds, stems and seeds, as the bulbs are inedible. Harvest the fronds throughout the summer months, and the stalks and seeds toward the end of the summer.

Use the fronds as a herb. Finely chop and add to fish dishes, potatoes and salads. Carrots sautéd in butter, salt, sugar and fennel fronds are delicious. The stems can be used to flavour vinegars and oils, or place them into your barbecue or campfire to smoke fish cooked on the grill above. You can grind the seeds into a powder and use them in Italian or Indian dishes. They even work well in sweet treats, such as biscuits.

Sorrel

Sorrel has a sharp, citrusy flavour, almost like apple. It can be used as a garnish, a salad leaf or cooked like spinach. It adds zing to soups and stews, and also makes a great ingredient in sweet recipes, such as cakes and sorbets.

Look for wild sorrel in parks, fields and lawns – almost anywhere grass grows. It's very common and easy to spot from spring onward, although it's available all year round. The only time you might have trouble finding it is during harsh winters or very hot, dry summers.

Sorrel's oval-shaped green leaf can be recognized by the two lobes at the base, which point downward. It has small red and green flower stalks that appear from May to August, and it grows upright to 60 centimetres (24 inches) in height. Toward the end of the summer, the leaves may be tinged with red, while red flowers and seeds grow on slender spikes.

Any sorrel leaves can be eaten, but the ones on the flower stems can be a little bitter. Pick the younger, more delicate leaves for salads.

NATURE IS NOT A PLACE
TO VISIT. IT IS HOME.

Gary Snyder

CAMPING ACTIVITIES

Anyone who's ever been camping knows that nature is one giant playground, so get active, play games, explore and discover. It doesn't matter how you camp, be it caravan, camper van or tent, whether it's day or night, sunny or raining – there are so many things to do when you're out in the wild. Why not take the opportunity to try something you've never done before, such as kayaking or rock climbing, learn a new skill, like rock skimming or whittling, or simply bathe in a forest and soak up nature? The following pages are brimming with ideas on how to keep occupied in the great outdoors.

FOREST BATHING

Shinrin-yoku, or forest bathing, simply refers to the practice of immersing yourself in nature. You're not walking for exercise, so slow down and take time to soak up the wonders of the natural world around you. Notice the way the light filters through the branches, listen to the echoes of birdsong, smell the earth, the plants and the rain, and feel the breeze on your face.

Forest bathing was developed in Japan in the 1980s, following studies into its benefits. Indeed, research shows that the practice reduces stress, depression and anxiety, as well as improving concentration, boosting the immune system and helping you get a good night's sleep. Here are some top tips, to help you make the most of your time among the trees.

HOW TO FOREST BATHE

Go at a quiet time of day. Try early morning or late evening. If you're going with a friend, agree not to talk until you finish your forest-bathing session.

Switch your phone off. Cleanse yourself of digital distractions, so you can be fully present in the moment.

Take your time. Pause now and then to take in the little things: the veins on a leaf; the feel of rough bark on your hand; the sound of the leaves as they rustle in the breeze. Use all of your senses.

Breathe. Close your eyes, relax and clear your mind. Focus only on your surroundings.

Leave any goals or expectations behind. Simply wander slowly, allowing your feet to carry you wherever they wish to go.

Stay for however long is right for you. Even just 10 minutes will leave you feeling cleansed.

WALKING

Walking is one of the most underrated forms of exercise. It might not be as intense a workout as running, but simply getting outside and putting one foot in front of the other has been shown to have some pretty impressive mental and physical health benefits.

Walking can reduce symptoms of depression, lower blood pressure, lessen the risk of heart disease and strokes, reduce cholesterol and help you lose weight. A great thing about walking is that it's low impact, so it's perfect for those with back, knee or ankle problems.

Surprisingly, there are many different ways to head for a walk. Take a leisurely stroll, aim for a steady pace, or speed it up and make it brisk. You can choose power walking, Nordic walking, race walking or even marathon walking.

The shorter days of winter needn't put a stop to your walks. Night walking is a powerful way to reconnect with nature – go with a friend for company and safety. With your vision reduced, your other senses become sharpened. After the sun sets, strap a head torch on and venture out into the countryside, walk across a deserted beach, follow the curve of a moonlit river or explore the shade of a wooded glade. In the dark, you'll experience the world anew: see if you can spot owls or bats beneath starlit skies, and listen for the calls of the night as you breathe in the crisp air.

BIRDWATCHING

If the idea of slowing down and connecting with the natural world sounds appealing, birdwatching could be your ideal outdoor activity. Witnessing a bird in its natural environment can leave you feeling relaxed and happy, due to birdwatching's meditative nature: intentionally spotting birds forces you to live completely in the present moment – waiting, watching and listening.

With more than 10,000 species of birds the world over, you'll never be far from some feathered friends, wherever you happen to be camping! So, whether it's wood pigeons on the lawn or buzzards soaring high above a mountain range, keep your eyes peeled.

You don't need to know anything about birds to enjoy watching them, but the more you spot, the better you will become at identifying them. A great way to start is by visiting a nature reserve, where you can see birds easily at close range.

DOS AND DON'TS

Do talk to others. Most birdwatchers enjoy sharing their knowledge. For many, a sense of community is an important part of birdwatching.

≫——▶

Do use your ears. Many birds are most easily identified by their song. Nightingales are famous for theirs, but often hide away inside bushes. Chiffchaffs and willow warblers look very similar, but their songs are distinctive.

≫——▶

Don't worry if you haven't got the latest gear – binoculars or spotting scopes can be useful, but aren't essential. In fact, you don't need expensive equipment to spot birds – all you need are your eyes and ears.

≫——▶

Do share your sightings. There are various apps and websites, such as BirdTrack, where you can log your sightings, helping experts to keep track of bird populations and contributing to their protection.

≫——▶

Don't disturb birds or their habitats. You might scare birds away from their nests, leaving chicks vulnerable.

CLOUD WATCHING

On a hillside, at the beach or just outside your tent, take a soft blanket or find a comfy patch of grass, lie down and simply watch as the clouds float by. You might be surprised at the variety you see. Some are white and fluffy, like cotton wool, others are grey and thin, while some tower high into the sky. Notice the colours. You may see white, grey, pink, purple or even gold. Each and every cloud is unique and is constantly evolving, and each catches the light in its own way.

COMMON CLOUDS:

CIRRUS: Delicate, wispy clouds found at high altitudes. Cirrus resembles strands of hair.

ALTOSTRATUS: Large, featureless, mid-level sheets of thin cloud. Altostratus is usually thin enough to just about see the sun through.

ALTOCUMULUS: Clumps of small, mid-level clouds, called cloudlets.

CUMULONIMBUS: Dense, towering clouds, formed by powerful upward air currents. They are white or grey, and in a storm they are known as thunderheads.

CUMULUS: Cumulus clouds have a flat base, and are puffy and cotton-like. These are the perfect fluffy clouds you'll see on a sunny day.

STRATOCUMULUS: Patches of low-level cloud that vary in colour, from bright white to dark grey.

STRATUS: Hazy, featureless, low-altitude clouds that vary in colour from dark to light grey. You'll see this on a typically overcast day. At ground level, we call stratus fog or mist.

SCAVENGER HUNT

A fun-filled game that can be played either on a campsite or while exploring out and about, a scavenger hunt is an activity in which the organizer prepares a list of items to be "hunted". The first person to find all the things on the list is the winner. It's a great game for both adults and children alike, and is the perfect way to get moving, learning and having fun together.

All you need for a scavenger hunt is you, but if you have a pen and paper you could write or draw a list of different things to look for. This will give you a purpose in your exploration. To mix things up a bit, you might want to take photographs of listed items, or set challenges to complete a list of tasks. Here are some ideas you might like to try:

- ▲ Challenges: stand on a tree stump, skim a stone, climb a tree, cross a stream without getting wet feet.

- ▲ Alphabet hike: find items with names that begin with each letter of the alphabet, from A to Z.

- ▲ Texture quest: find something rough, smooth, squelchy, prickly.

- ▲ Rubbings: make leaf rubbings of oak, pine, sycamore.

- ▲ Riddles: write clues about the items you'll be looking for.

LIVE ALL YOU CAN;
IT'S A MISTAKE NOT TO.

Henry James

WILD SWIMMING

Swimming outdoors is a great way to connect with nature, and is thought to have a multitude of mental and physical health benefits. Apart from the immense euphoria you'll feel, open-water swimming has been shown to reduce symptoms of depression, ease chronic pain and even slow the onset of dementia.

You can seek out idyllic wild swimming spots the world over, from secret beaches to epic lakes and crystal-clear rivers. If you're new to wild swimming, start in summer when the water is a little warmer. You might want to wear a wetsuit, to keep warm and for added buoyancy, as well as neoprene shoes and gloves.

TOP TIPS

Check the current: throw a stick into the water. If it floats away faster than you can swim, you won't be able to swim against the current.

»———→

Get in slowly: if the water is cold (and you might be surprised how chilly it can be, even on a warm day), you will experience the "cold shock response". This is an instinctive gasp. If you jump or dive in and your airway is underwater when you gasp, you risk swallowing enough water to drown.

»———→

Know when to get out: hypothermia creeps up on you. Look for the "umbles" – fumbling, grumbling, stumbling and mumbling. These are all signs it's time to get out and warm up.

»———→

Don't swim alone: you'll be able to spot if your friend is getting too cold or in trouble – and they can do the same for you.

STARGAZING

On a clear, dark night, turn off any lights, grab a blanket and a cosy jumper, and head outside. Then lie back, look up and lose yourself in the wondrous canopy of space above: nothing on Earth can give you a more powerful sense of cosmic scale. The realization that we're nothing but specks on a rock, tumbling around our yellow sun – one of countless stars spiralling the Milky Way – can be immensely liberating. And remember – our galaxy is just one of many that makes up the universe. The longer you gaze, the more stars you'll discover.

Top five constellations to spot:

- ▲ Ursa Major, the Great Bear
- ▲ Ursa Minor, the Little Bear
- ▲ Orion, the Hunter
- ▲ Taurus, the Bull
- ▲ Gemini, the Twins

CAMPFIRE GAMES

When the sun is low and you're huddled by the campfire, why not play some games? Here are a few ideas that will have your friends and family getting creative, being silly and making precious memories until long after bedtime.

I SPY

Everyone knows how to play I spy, but camping I spy is more challenging as there are only so many objects you can see and make people guess at! After a short while, you have to get really inventive: D for damp patch, for instance, or I for inflatable dog bowl...

HAPPY CAMPERS

Make sure you have some sheets of paper and pens. Give them out to each camper. Fold the paper into three. Everyone draws the head of a typical happy camper on the first third of paper. Then they fold the paper over, so no one can see what they've drawn. Everyone passes their paper on and then draws a torso, folding that over and passing the paper on. Finally, everyone draws the legs. When it's complete, reveal the happy camper you've drawn... weird and wonderful results guaranteed!

ONCE UPON A CAMPSITE

This is a storytelling game. Appoint one member of the group as story editor. They choose the theme of the story. The first person then tells the first three sentences of a story, starting with "Once upon a campsite". The

editor then selects the next person to introduce the first character, and that person adds three sentences. Next, the editor selects another person to add an additional character/an event/a twist, and so on, until the story is finished. The best part is, it can be as short or as long as you want!

WHAT AM I?

Simple but fun. One person thinks of an object or animal, then each member of the group is allowed three questions to try to work out what it is.

SPOT THE DIFFERENCE

Gather together as much of your smaller camping gear as you can and place it in the centre of the tent. Once done, the group can spend ten seconds looking at it, then they have to turn around. Remove one item. When the group turns back, they must try to work out what's missing.

BANFF NATIONAL PARK, CANADA

Every year, millions of visitors travel to the Canadian Rockies, to wonder at the jagged peaks of the Icefields Parkway, Lake Louise's emerald waters and the glistening Athabasca Glacier.

Banff National Park is situated in the ecoregion of the Alberta Mountain forests. It began life as a 26-square-kilometre (10-square-mile) hot-springs reserve and has grown into 6,641 square kilometres (2,564 square miles) of unparalleled mountain scenery.

In winter, get your adrenaline hit by skiing Mount Norquay, while in summer months you can enjoy mountain hiking or biking trails, or take to the water by rafting, canoeing or fishing.

WILD CAMPING

Are you looking for adventure? If you want to leave your normal life behind and totally immerse yourself in nature, far from civilization of any kind (even a campsite), wild camping could be exactly what you need. But don't just drop everything and run off into the wilderness. The following chapter details some top tips that will ensure your wild camping trip runs smoothly. Get reading, and you'll be fully prepared, know the dos and don'ts, understand how to choose the perfect spot and how to pitch up, as well as how to camp legally and safely.

WHAT IS WILD CAMPING?

Wild camping involves sleeping in the wilderness, rather than at a campsite or caravan park. It is one of the few things you can do in this life that will give the feeling of complete freedom, setting off on your own two feet, with only what you can carry on your back and the wind for company. You might want to set off on a multi-day hike and pitch camp wherever you find yourself along the way when the sun sets, or you could try a micro adventure, leaving real life for a short while and sleeping in nature for just one night.

Tempting though it is to just up and leave, it's important to do your research. Wild camping is only allowed in certain places, so always find out where and when you can camp legally.

WILD CAMPING ETIQUETTE

Here are some top tips for wild camping, to ensure you camp safely and respectfully:

- ▲ Tell someone before you leave. Let them know where you are going and for how long.

- ▲ Make sure you're prepared for all weather conditions.

- ▲ Arrive late and leave early: wild camping is intended for sleeping at night only.

- ▲ Always ensure there aren't any "no camping" signs before pitching your tent.

- ▲ Don't start a fire unless it's safe to do so and be sure to monitor it at all times. Make sure it's completely extinguished when you leave.

- ▲ When making a toilet hole, first check there are no water sources nearby. Dig so that it's approximately 15 centimetres (6 inches) deep. Cover it up and take your toilet roll with you when you leave.

- ▲ Be considerate of the nature, animals and people around you. If asked to move on, do so quickly and politely.

- ▲ Be inconspicuous – when you leave, there should be no trace of your presence.

CHOOSING YOUR PITCH

If it's your first time to a particular area, there's no need to worry. With the help of a map, you can often pick out a great pitch before you even lay eyes on it in real life.

HOW TO CHOOSE THE PERFECT SPOT

1. Look for somewhere away from towns and villages – you want to make sure you're staying well away from people's gardens. Lots of green on the map is a good sign.

2. You'll need a good water source nearby – look for rivers, which are shown by blue lines.

3. Now you need a way in – look for broken lines on your map, which indicate footpaths or bridleways. You'll need to pitch at least 50 metres (164 feet) from them, but they are useful for getting you into wilder spaces – especially at night.

4. Check out the contours – many maps will include lines marked with numbers; these indicate the height of the land you'll be walking on. The closer together and more tightly clustered these are, the steeper the ground rises. The further apart, the gentler the slope. You'll want as flat a ground as possible, so wide gaps in the contours are what you're looking for.

5. Know your symbols – watch out for symbols that indicate soggy and boggy ground, not good for pitching a tent and usually a breeding ground for midges, so best avoided. Also, look out for the symbol for boulder fields. Again, not good for a sleeping mat!

You can always check out your chosen spot on Google Earth before you go, or look at photographs of the general area. The important thing is to have a couple of backup spots prepared, in case your first choice turns out to be unsuitable, or there's someone else already there!

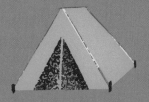

PITCHING TIPS

SOLID GROUND

You won't get a good night's sleep if you end up on uneven ground, so before you position the tent, lie down on the ground first to check it's a comfortable spot, free from hidden holes, lumps and bumps, or big rocks. You will rarely get a completely flat piece of ground to pitch on, but remember that on a slope – even a slight one – you need to keep your head uphill and your feet downhill, especially if there's more than one of you. You don't want to find yourselves sliding out of bed sideways and ending up in a heap at one end of the tent!

CHECK THE WIND DIRECTION

High winds can not only make your tent fabric flap and keep you up at night, but they can also loosen guy lines, with the result that you have to keep getting up to readjust them throughout your stay. Position your tent so that the sharpest corner (perhaps a pole that juts out) faces the wind, to help break it. If at all possible, keep your tent entrance away from the prevailing wind. Also, when pegging out your tent, position the guy lines into the wind and try to achieve a 90-degree angle between the lines and the pegs.

WILDERNESS IS NOT A
LUXURY BUT A NECESSITY
OF THE HUMAN SPIRIT.

Edward Abbey

THINGS TO DO BEFORE YOU GO

Taking that first step into the wild can be daunting. Beyond the canvas door of your tent, there's no campsite shop where you can buy everything you forgot to pack, no receptionist to give you directions, no water on tap and no campsite neighbours to ask for help. If you feel fully prepared before you go, you'll be able to enjoy the feeling of being wild and free without worry. Here are some things to consider:

- ▲ Research your area before you go, so you can be prepared for all eventualities.

- ▲ Check the weather. If it looks like rain, don't forget your waterproof gear. If it will be cold, it's worth making space in your luggage for some extra layers.

- ▲ While it's important to bring enough provisions and equipment to keep you safe and healthy, you do also have to carry everything, so travel as lightly as you can.

- ▲ Consider your food. If you want hot meals, then ensure you have a stove that's lightweight and portable. Otherwise, stick with cold, pre-prepared items.

- ▲ Minimize potential for litter before you set off, as you have to carry this with you, too. For instance, decant any food in containers and bin the packaging before your trip. You could also bring extra bags, to hold any rubbish that you end up with.

ALL GOOD THINGS
ARE WILD AND FREE

BIVOUACKING

Fancy drifting off under a ceiling of stars and waking as the sun's rays appear over the horizon? Bivouacking – sleeping outside without a tent – really is the ultimate in overnight outdoor adventures. It can include anything from bedding down on a sandy beach to securing yourself to a cliff ledge during a two-day climb to the summit.

Bivouacking is like camping and then some. You can enjoy all the same benefits, but to a greater extent, as it allows you to feel closer to nature and you're able to reach even wilder places.

In warm weather, you need nothing more than the clothes you're wearing. However, temperatures can drop at night even in the summer, so you might want a few bits of kit that will make your stay a little more comfortable – a sleeping bag, mat and bivvy bag (a waterproof bag you sleep inside).

TOP TIPS

Synthetic sleeping bags dry faster and keep you warm even when wet.

»———→

Choose a foam mat. An inflatable one won't provide you with insulation from a cold floor.

»———→

Wear a woolly hat to keep your head warm at night.

»———→

Don't bivouac where there is a risk of falling rocks or rising waters.

»———→

Find your spot before sunset, so you can survey the area for comfort and safety.

»———→

Don't leave any leftovers, as food could attract animals.

»———→

Pack up your belongings before you go to sleep, to protect them from the morning dew.

THE LAKE DISTRICT, UNITED KINGDOM

The Lake District National Park, in north-west England, is world-famous for its lakes, fells and glacial dales. This UNESCO World Heritage Site is a popular playground for walkers and outdoor enthusiasts alike. Try gorge walking, canoeing, sailing, kayaking, rock climbing, abseiling, mountain biking and, of course, hiking.

   Wild camping here is only permitted above the highest fell wall (approximately 400 metres/1,300 feet) and if there are already two tents in one area, you will need to move on and find somewhere else. There is a huge choice of campsites, however, and plenty that can offer the simplicity and tranquility of a remote valley or secluded lake shore.

FINLAND

Finland might just be the best place in
the world to go wild camping. This beautiful
country is full of lakes and other water sources,
and is home to some of the most welcoming people you
could meet. Wild camping in Finland is not just legal – on both
public and private land – but enshrined in law as a right for everyone
to enjoy. In the roadless wilds of northern and eastern Finland, open wilderness
huts are available to rest for the night. The huts are free to use, but be prepared
to share with other hikers and, before you leave, get some firewood ready for the
next occupant.

CARAVANS AND CAMPER VANS

From giant, house-sized caravans to pop-up campers, the range of caravans and camper vans available to choose from is enormous. Read on to discover why you might wish to choose caravanning or camper-vanning, some top tips and bucket-list trips, whether to rent or buy, and how to do it in style.

THE JOY OF CARAVANNING

For many, caravanning and camper-vanning is not just about going on holiday: it's a way of life. There is an affinity between caravanners and camper-vanners – a little nod when you pass on the road, a chat over the campsite water tap, and a desire to support each other with advice or a helping hand.

This kind of camping offers a great chance to relax and enjoy being in nature, while still benefiting from many of the comforts of home – including a TV, sofa, fridge and nice warm bed. Caravans and camper vans give you the freedom to explore at your own pace, then park up and chill out with very little effort.

RENTING YOUR RIDE

You don't need to own your own vehicle to enjoy caravanning or camper-vanning – by renting, anyone can enjoy the freedom of the open road. Hiring can also be the perfect way to try out different styles of accommodation, before you do take the plunge and buy. Want to get to grips with it all? Here's some caravanning and camper-vanning lingo to listen out for:

TWIN-AXLE CARAVANS have four wheels. They are typically heavier than a single-axle caravan and are more stable on the road.

TEARDROP TRAILERS are streamlined, compact and lightweight.

POP-TOP CARAVANS AND CAMPER VANS have a roof that pops up to offer standing room.

FOLDING CARAVANS reduce drag when you're driving, so increase fuel economy, stability and driver visibility.

AIRSTREAM CARAVANS are the classic American brand of caravan, easily recognized by their distinctive rounded shape and polished aluminium body.

CAMPER VANS are a self-contained, self-propelled travelling home!

My wish is to stay always like this, living quietly in a corner of nature.

CLAUDE MONET

TOP TIPS FOR STRESS-FREE TRIPS

Here are some of the things you might want to think about before you hit the road, to ensure a smooth, stress-free trip:

▲ To make sure all your belongings get through the trip in one piece, write a checklist of things that need to be secured or tidied away before you drive.

▲ Learn the size of your caravan – write down the dimensions and put them somewhere you'll see them (in both feet and metres), so that when you get to a low tunnel or a narrow lane, you can drive through with confidence.

▲ Check for any tollbooths you might encounter on your route. If you'll be going through any, consider having some change handy – they may not take cards.

▲ Keep the camper van or caravan manual to hand, in case of any problems.

▲ Before you leave, write down the details of local mechanics, you might need one at short notice.

▲ Plan ahead for petrol and take a spare can with you. It's worth having a spare tyre or puncture repair kit, too.

▲ Drive safely – caravans can be tricky to handle. Take your time when driving, check your mirrors twice as often as you normally would, and take extra care if you're overtaking.

CAMPER-VAN ROAD TRIPS OF THE WORLD

From the epic classics to the road less travelled, here are some ultimate road trips around the world that should definitely be at the top of every camper-vanner's bucket list!

HIGHWAY 101, CALIFORNIA
USA

NORTH COAST
500
SCOTLAND

SNÆFELLSNES
PENINSULA
ICELAND

OKAHANDJA
TO ETOSHA
NATIONAL
PARK
NAMIBIA

THE GREAT
ALPINE
HIGHWAY
NEW ZEALAND

AYUTTHAYA TO
CHIANG MAI
THAILAND

PAN-AMERICAN
HIGHWAY
NORTH AND
SOUTH AMERICA

ASHINOKO
AND HAKONE
SKYLINE
COURSE
JAPAN

THE CAMBRIAN
WAY
WALES

ALSACE WINE
ROUTE
FRANCE

CAMPING HACKS

Forgotten your mosquito repellent? Light a fire to keep the little blighters away. Is the weather going to be hot, hot, hot? Freeze your food and drink before you go to keep it fresh and cold for longer. Airbeds can be chilly to sleep on, so put a blanket underneath your sleeping bag for some much-needed extra insulation. Let solar-powered fairy lights take the slack, in case of torch failure. There are so many tricks to keep your camping trip running smoothly, even when things are not going to plan. Here are some other top camping hacks every camper should know...

DUCT TAPE TO THE RESCUE

It's well worth taking a roll of duct tape on your trip, because it's great for patching up practically anything. Hole in your backpack? Torn clothes? Broken saucepan handle? Leaky water bottle? Collapsing tent? Nothing a bit of duct tape can't fix.

DAYLIGHT MEASURE

Did you know you can estimate the amount of daylight left using nothing more than your bare hand? Hold your arm parallel to the horizon with your fingers straight and your thumb tucked in. Line up your index finger with the bottom of the sun, then count how many finger widths there are between the sun and the horizon. Each finger equals roughly 15 minutes of daylight. (Note: this only works if you are in the mid-latitudes.)

TICK-REPELLENT SPRAY

Nobody likes to come home from a trip in the outdoors only to find they've been bitten by a tick. To prevent this critter from getting to you, use this tick-repellent hack. Put one part tea-tree oil and two parts water into a spray bottle. Spritz the mixture onto your clothes, shoes and tent, and the ticks will head elsewhere for their lunch.

TAPE TRAIL

If you're walking in dense forest, getting back to your campsite again can be a challenge. Instead of worrying about getting lost, try this simple hack. Use brightly coloured biodegradable tape to mark out your route. Leave small tabs in easy-to-spot places, or if you're really in the thick of it, and you're not going very far, run a longer stretch of tape out at waist height. Remember to remove the tape on your return trip.

BOTTLE BOOST

Many campers will already have a stainless-steel water bottle, and it might also be double-skinned, which helps to insulate the contents. But you can make it even better with this hack! Wrapping your bottle in duct tape will give it an extra layer of insulation and increase its performance. In cold weather, it will also protect your fingers from a chill when holding the bottle.

KEEPING THINGS COOL

If you've purified your water by boiling it, but want to drink it quickly, take it to a nearby stream. Wedge the container firmly between stones and allow the cold water to rush over it. After a few minutes, it should be cool enough to drink.

ALL I NEED IS A CAMPSITE
AND GOOD COMPANY

FOR-THE-WIN WELLIES

If you forget to pack your wellies, or they break midway through your trip, here's a hack to help keep your feet dry.

WHAT YOU NEED:

4–6 plastic bags (without holes)

Duct tape

A small pair of scissors

HOW TO MAKE THEM:

1. First, put your shoes on. Then put each foot inside a plastic bag. Tie the handles firmly around your ankles (though not so tightly that you cut off your circulation).

2. Take two more plastic bags and cut a hole in the bottom of each one that's big enough to slide your foot through. Put each bag around your leg like a leg warmer and tie the handles in a knot. Depending on how tall you are, and how much coverage you want, you may have to repeat this step further up your calves.

3. Next, wind duct tape around each leg, starting at your toes and finishing where the plastic bags meet your flesh or clothes. Remember to add extra tape where the plastic bags join together and where the makeshift boots end. This will give you extra waterproof protection.

4. Now you can do whatever you had planned, without the weather stopping you.

STRIKE ME LUCKY

Taking matches on a camping trip is essential, but the abrasive pads on matchboxes can be a bit temperamental and won't always work if conditions are soggy. To insure against this, take a strip of sandpaper to use instead, which works just as well. You could even use a nail file if you want your luggage to be as multifunctional as possible!

BOTTLE ILLUMINATOR

Here's how to create your very own free-standing lamp. Pack a large water bottle and a head torch with an elastic strap/headband. When it gets dark, secure the torch to the water bottle using its strap, so the light is facing inward, and voilà – you can illuminate the whole tent or area.

COMFY MATTRESS

For a comfier night's sleep, try this hack. Bring along some interlocking foam floor tiles (the ones that are used in children's nurseries) or a couple of yoga mats. Place these on the bottom of the tent for extra padding, and put your sleeping bag on top.

EMERGENCY CRAYONS

A steady source of light is key when you're hiking or camping. If you find yourself without a torch, this hack can be useful. Wax crayons with paper casings can be lit like candles, and are great when there are no other light sources to hand. You can usually get up to half an hour's light from a lit crayon.

LUGGAGE TIP

If you're travelling with another person, coordinate your packing so you don't take more than you need. For instance, share items such as a hairbrush, sun cream and toothpaste, all of which you'll both be using. This is especially good for those who are going wild camping and need to travel light.

DRY BOOTS

Nobody likes to have wet shoes! This hack will help to dry out your boots after a hard day of hiking in the rain. Screw up some balls of newspaper and stuff them loosely into your wet shoes. The paper will absorb the moisture and dry your boots out much quicker than heat alone. Replace the paper after a couple of hours.

TOASTY SLEEPING BAG

If a cold night is on the cards, give your sleeping bag a boost by using heat reflectors – the kind that people often put in their car windows. By slipping one into your sleeping bag, you'll create a layer of heat-reflecting insulation to keep you toasty.

FIRELIGHTER

If you want a barbecue on your trip, this is two hacks in one. For a barbecue, you need fuel – but don't lug a heavy bag of charcoal with you. Instead, pack pieces individually into egg cartons. Not only is this easier and safer to carry, but the egg carton acts as a firelighter. All you have to do is light the cardboard, and the fire will catch on to the charcoal.

GET BUSY WITH BEESWAX

Waterproofing your gear is an essential precaution for any trek. However, most spray-on proofers are made up of synthetic chemicals, which aren't good for the environment. So try this natural alternative: beeswax! Beeswax is actually used in many proofing products, but it can also be used in its pure form. Simply rub it directly onto garments, bags and shoes.

TENT-ROPE IDENTIFIER

Use this hack to make your tent easier to find in the dark. Take several swim noodles and cut them the same length as each of your tent ropes. With a penknife, make a vertical slit down one whole side of each of the noodles. Finally, slot the noodles onto the ropes. Your tent is now easier to find, plus you'll reduce your chance of tripping over the ropes and having an accident. Win-win!

DELICIOUS MEALS

Herbs and spices can take your campsite cooking to the next level. While you can't take the whole spice rack with you on your trip, you could use mint tins to take small portions of your favourite seasonings.

CONCLUSION

Life is better when you're camping. Camping is freedom. It's letting go of all your usual ties, and thinking only about the here and now.

Camping is a star-filled night, the warm glow of embers, the smell of earth crushed underfoot. The simplicity of life outdoors helps us to appreciate the little things, while being at the mercy of nature reminds us of our place in the universe.

Camping is the place where strangers become friends and memories last forever – on the campsite, stargazing from the door of your two-man tent, parked up in a luxury motorhome, or snuggled into a bivvy bag on the side of a wild and windy mountain. Your great outdoor adventure can be whatever you want it to be. Maybe you'll want to try something new, such as foraging, bushcraft or wild camping. With all your newly gained tips and tricks, you'll be camping like a pro, whichever way you decide to do it.

Hopefully, within these pages you've found the inspiration to get out there with confidence. When you strip away the phones, the jobs, the decor and the possessions, we are all just wild souls. So trade those four walls for a couple of tent poles and a canvas. You won't regret it. After all, home is where the heart is, and your heart is in the wilderness.

IMAGE CREDITS

Have you enjoyed this book? If so, find us on Facebook at
Summersdale Publishers, on Twitter at **@Summersdale** and
on Instagram at **@summersdalebooks** and get in touch.
We'd love to hear from you!

www.summersdale.com